CHRISTIAN VITALITY PRAYER

ACHIEVING CHRISTIAN VITALITY AND

ABUNDANCE THROUGH PRAYER

By

DAN MATEJSEK

Copyright © 2014 Christian Vitality LLC. All rights reserved worldwide. Permission is granted for quotations in all manner of religious assembly.

ISBN-13:978-0692351161

Scripture taken from the English Standard Version®, The Voice® and The Message®. Copyright © The Zondervan Corporation, L.L.C. Used by permission. All rights reserved.

Christian Vitality™, Soul Conditioning™, Real-Time Living™, and Victories In Progress™ are trademarks of Christian Vitality LLC. All rights reserved.

ChristianVitality.com/Free-Bonuses
$97 Value - (PASSWORD=revival)

facebook.com/ChristianVitalityPrayerBook

Dedication

To God: Thank you for being my best friend in good and bad times. Thank you for entrusting me with the stewardship of these revelations of wisdom that you've given me in prayer and your living word. May my work be worthy of your "Job well done, good and faithful servant" at the end of my life.

To Readers: May the Lord Jesus use the Christian Vitality Prayer to awaken and instill a dream so BIG for your life that only he can make it come true. May he also bless you richly and abundantly on your journey to fulfill God's perfect will for YOUR life. In Jesus' name, AMEN!

To Diana: For being my best friend in everything, in pursuit of a Christ-centered life and for your constant encouragement and support.

To Rachel, Jonathan, Ellie, Leo, and Grace: May my work for the Lord make you proud some day, but more importantly may it lead you closer in your own relationship with Jesus Christ.

Preface

Dear Sister/Brother,

Thank you for investing in yourself and purchasing this book/program. If it were up to me, I would have given it to you for free as I believe I am simply a steward of the revelations of wisdom that God has given me to assemble this for you. Unfortunately, getting the word out costs lots of money these days. I have to charge for this book/program quite simply so I can afford to get it in front of more believers. Just know that your money is going towards introducing this little miracle to another believer down the line. Similarly, if you find it would be a blessing to a family member or loved one, I would be honored if you would introduce it to them or even **buy them an Amazon gift card** to buy their own copy. Together we can start a revival in the body of believers that will help us achieve the great commission in a bigger and better way. After all, the greatest compliment any author receives from a reader is a referral. Thank you in advance.

My goal for this training is that it is received as something beautifully inspiring. I hope you will not only go through this training and get warm fuzzies and an uplift in your prayer life (and life overall) for the moment, but that you will take action on this material today and integrate it into your life long term. **My goal is to help YOU produce a life change in and for you—one that would allow you to increase your level of maturity in Christ and increase your level of Christian Vitality & Abundance. A Revival.**

I believe God's greatest expression of his love to humanity is allowing us a free will. A will free to choose -- to choose him, to choose to have an abundant life or a life of lack, to choose his plan for our lives or the plan of the enemy, and to choose to follow the teachings of Jesus Christ or follow the ways of the world. Thank you for exercising your free will in your purchase, but more importantly, please do so and take action on what this book reveals to you. I sincerely know that if you do, you will bring about a revival in your life—your Spiritual life, your Soul, and your Body.

Please join me in applying this prayer to your life today. Don't file it away to be forgotten. You are worth it. After all, **God made you, Christ saved you, and that, my sister or brother, makes YOU a believer of TREMENDOUS worth.** You are a Vital Christian to God's mission and purposes on earth.

When you use and affirm the Christian Vitality Prayer, it will start to change your thoughts. Your thoughts will then start to change your beliefs. Your beliefs will start to change your expectations. Your expectations will then change your actions, and your actions will then change your outcomes. Everything in your life will start to align with God's will for your life, and I believe you'll experience a revival in all areas of your life.

Romans 8:28 (ESV) says "And we know that for those who love God all things work together for good, for those who are called according to his purpose."

I am going to boldly proclaim that God is calling you to a greater purpose in your life—one that requires you to make changes in how you approach your spiritual, physical, and mental health.

Christian Vitality is not a destination. It is a journey, and when you achieve it, your adventure finally begins. You then become the hero who has achieved this great transformation. You are sent off into the world on your own individual mission to help bring other believers to the promise of being a Vital Christian and fulfilling God's mission in your life—one who lives their life on purpose at a capacity of service that was never before been possible.

May the Lord Jesus use the Christian Vitality Prayer to awaken and instill a dream so BIG for your life that only he can make it come true. May he also bless you richly and abundantly on your journey to fulfill God's perfect will for YOUR life. In Jesus' name, AMEN!

Sincerely and faithfully yours,

Pastor Dan Matejsek

Pastor Dan Matejsek, AE, BS, EIT, CPT, CSNC

Ordained Christian Minister (License #689912412)

Table of Contents

Dedication

Preface

Chapter 1. Encounter God Every Day!

Chapter 2. The Need for Prayer

Chapter 3. Christian Vitality Defined

Chapter 4. Answering Some Possible Objections to Using the Christian Vitality Prayer

Chapter 5. The Christian Vitality Prayer

Chapter 6. How to Stop Worrying the Christian Way

Chapter 7. Start YOUR Prayer-Powered Life Revival Today

CHAPTER 8. What to do Once You Receive Your Big Dream

About the Author

Read These Other Prayer Books

Chapter 1. Encounter God Every Day!

The Christian Vitality Prayer has absolutely changed my life on all levels. To give you a glimpse of my prayer and my vision for how it will impact you personally, I'll share with you a personal experience of what it has done for me in my life. In doing so, I pray that it instills a desire in you that is sufficient to motivate you to take action on what you'll learn in this book. I hope you say, "I want that in my life too, Lord."

I'll also share another affirmation/prayer that I use in addition to the Christian Vitality Prayer. You'll also learn a simple trick that Harvard research scientists have proved will benefit you in your prayer and worship life. So the story begins….

I started off my day much like any other by hopping straight out of bed half asleep with the temptation of my pillow calling my name. "Yell a loud No" James tells me (James 4:7 The Message). So, I ignored the calling of my comfortable little friend. "God's going to do some cool things today…gotta get to it," I told myself as I walked away from my bed.

I paused for a moment with arms outstretched to heaven (I stood as if being held up in a bank heist). I call this the Power Pose. I'll talk in more detail about the science behind why this has a huge impact on our bodies later. The short version is that Harvard doctors have proven that if you stand feet shoulder width apart, hands outstretched, and reach for the sky—then hold that for an extended amount of time (two or more minutes)—it will actually change your body's chemistry. The hormones that produce the feelings of **power, confidence, and certainty** will go up in your body. I do this throughout the day when I feel fatigued and tired, and it works like a charm. Is it coincidental that the Bible suggests that we lift up our hands to heaven? I don't think so. Now science proves it is good for us. Go figure. Yet another ancient biblical principal proven by science to be good for us.

With eyes closed and an open heart, I say the Christian Vitality Prayer (this is only a portion of it, the rest of the prayer is in Chapter 5): Oh God, Creator and Sustainer of the whole Universe, YOU are MY loving Father and interested in every detail of my life. You only have GOOD for ME and desire to give me healing, wholeness, and forgiveness. Everything over which You've given ME authority I place at YOUR feet.

I then rattled off all the things that may tempt me to worry on any given day. They were all his now to worry about and take care of, releasing me of the responsibility. There was an immense amount of freedom to be had there.

Diana and I are the stewards of five beautiful little people whom we love very much. This comes with the responsibility of making sure they have breakfast and lunch for the day.

Being a school day, that was my mission of the moment.

So, careful not to stumble while walking with only one eye open, I made my way down the stairs to the kitchen to get breakfast and school lunches ready.

I'd been at this place spiritually, mentally, and physically where I felt I was closer to God than I had ever been. The Christian Vitality Prayer combined with the Power Pose and another affirmation are what I give credit to for this phenomenal life experience.

Not out of a religious habit or in a manipulative way, I was verbalizing this to God, myself, and the kitchen cabinets:

"Thank you, God, for this place you brought me to. I don't want this feeling to ever end."

I'd been feeling a sense of synchronicity (like God was laying out every step of the day to work for my good, not in a selfish "I want this" or "I want that way"). I took one step and then another. Sometimes the step I took didn't make sense, but by the end of the day or the end of the week, it seemed they were all well laid out plans for his purposes in my life to prevail. It was as though like every detail of my life was part of his plan and on purpose.

There's a song inspired by scripture that describes God being a lamp unto my feet. Well, what most people don't know is that in ancient times, they actually wore little lamps around their feet at night that would light each step they took. Unlike today's flood lamps, those lamps of ancient times forced them to take one step at a time. This synchronicity is like that. I just take what I feel are Spirit-led steps (fully surrendered to God's will in the moment), and God takes care of the rest. I focus solely in that moment…in the now…in the present moment. This is exactly what I'll teach you here in this book.

Back to the moment in the kitchen now…so I had just finished telling God thank you for the place I was in. Then I felt a feeling of calmness, oneness, and then awareness when these words came out of my mouth:

"God, I appreciate you! [PAUSE] I'm proud of you!"

I started to tear up. I was overcome by that feeling of happiness experienced at a great movie with a happy ending. I realized that was the first time I had said those exact words. What you don't know, which brought even more meaning to me personally, is that four days prior I had that exact same moment with my oldest daughter, Rachel (twelve years old at that time).

We had one of those moments where I felt God was using me to speak truth into her life—words with deep meaning and hopefully long-lasting effects on her life. At the end of that forty-five minute talk she said:

"I'm proud of you, Dad. [PAUSE] I appreciate you!"

This was the first time she's ever told me that. Coincidentally, that morning was the first time I told God the Father essentially the same thing. I apologized to God and then told him, "Thank you, God, for revealing that to me today. I promise to share this epiphany with everyone you send my way and to do a better job of letting you know I'm proud of you and appreciate you."

Why not make every day a God appreciation day? Why don't we have a God appreciation day on the calendar...or a God appreciation week like the nurses, teachers, and office managers have? It likely won't ever happen on a national level-- that would be just too darn silly to those less enlightened ones. But for you and me, sister or brother, we can do it on a personal level every day. Please join me. Tell me by sending me an email about your encounter with God today: dan@christianvitality.com.

I believe at least part of the reason I am at this place of awareness of God's presence is, in addition to the Christian Vitality Prayer, I've also reintroduced a practice of saying an affirmation prayer I learned from Joseph Murphy in the book *Think Yourself Rich*. He's not a traditional pastor, and many Christians who have not read much about him may even think of him of as a person more on the outside of the Christian faith than on the inside. I'd disagree to some extent because I've read that book at least a dozen times, and it is full of Bible excerpts cover to cover. He was an expert on just about every human religion and, I believe, a fellow of many colleges when he passed away. He was also an expert on the subconscious mind and metaphysics. I believe by meditating on the Bible, every man or woman, independent of their religion, will be impacted by what Christians call God's living word (the Bible). I think he was also enlightened in this way.

I'm not suggesting you lead yourself astray by chasing after what some may call false prophets and adopting all of what Joseph Murphy reveals in that book. But if you feel yourself grounded in your Christian faith, at least allow yourself to be open to the fact that many scholars who study the Bible for many, many years are impacted in a profound way. What they share of what they learned has been touched by God through his living word.

That said, I want to reveal to you a practice I've reintroduced into my life. It has had an immense impact on my life and brought me to where I am today. I've reintroduced a prayer/affirmation that Joseph Murphy taught me, and I am currently saying it throughout the day. He instructed that you say it first thing in the morning when you get up and then say it a few times right before you go to sleep. The reason for this is that your subconscious mind is more open to suggestion (proven by science and research) at those times, and you can essentially reprogram your brain. I personally made it a prayer/affirmation and memorized it years ago. It goes like this:

"Right now, I am writing in my subconscious mind the idea of **God's** wealth. **God** is the source of **my** supply, and all my needs are met at every moment of time and point of space (circumstance). **God's** wealth flows freely, joyously, and ceaselessly into my experience and I thank **God** for his riches forever circulating into **my** life." – Joseph Murphy Ph.D., D.D. from *Think Yourself Rich* (I emphasize the bold words when I say it.)

Through the practice of praying this affirmation (in addition to the Christian Vitality Prayer) every day—morning and night (and even throughout the day)—I have reached a level of awareness, synchronicity, and oneness with God the Father. The Creator. The Sustainer of the Universe. I am so, so blessed and thankful.

So how do we encounter God EVERY day? Out of prayer and submission to him, I've been led (I believe divinely) to a practice that can be summarized with this acronym—SOAPP:

Synchronicity + Oneness + Awareness = (come from) Prayer + Power Pose

So, sister or brother, I challenge you today to integrate SOAPP into your life and watch your encounters with God come.

It is my sincere and genuine prayer that this message will be a blessing to you and your loved ones. May it allow God to use you in a bigger way in the circle of influence he's placed you in. In Jesus' name, AMEN!

Chapter 2. The Need for Prayer

Your Soul's Thirst to Be a Vital Christian on Fire for God

I hope you come to realize now, like I did, that you've been thinking too small and limiting the amount of God's wealth and abundance that can and will enter your life.

You can now have a degree of clarity and focus that makes you feel attuned to what God's purposes for your life are. This will allow you to operate in a place where you are truly and genuinely 100% you and 100% present in the moment while being the person God wants you to be and allowing yourself to be used by him to change the world we live in.

You can and will (if you follow the advice in this book) start to feel like you are on fire and in a permanent state of "flow". It will feel like you've been possessed by God and just need to step out of his way and let him do absolutely amazing things—things you could never do yourself—and start fulfilling a dream so big for your life that only God himself can make it happen.

You will be your only limitation if you let your "self" or your ego get in the way of what he has planned. I want you to commit to God to never again allow yourself to operate at the ground level of life. Instead, you will only operate in a place where you are flying high in the clouds on God's coattails. You'll have a significant impact on humanity by being 100% present at all times and 100% surrendered to the fact that God is your source and supply and guides you in all your steps, if you'll let him. That is what living a Vital Christian's life is all about…living with Christian Vitality.

Imagine what your life will be like when you've reached that level of awareness, synchronicity, and oneness with God the Father--when you truly feel in-step with God, the Creator, the Sustainer of the whole universe. Imagine having a powerful, empowering daily encounter with God, being flooded with a feeling of being blessed, and having confidence that God is laying out the steps you need to take on a daily basis…literally directing your path. It's a place of freedom to be 100% you while God is 100% in charge. The level of gratitude you'll feel will be overwhelming.

I think every believer wants to be that close to God, and if they had even a small taste of it, they would never want anything else.

The secret to having these powerful experiences is what this book is all about—laying out the foundation in prayer and affirmation so that you, too, can obtain this and become the empowered believer God wants you to be. The believer that deep down in your soul you thirst to become…that you need to become.

The Need for Regular Prayer and the Challenges Christians Face Today

According to a Pew Research Study in 2013, fifty-five percent of Americans said they pray every day. Twenty-three percent said they pray weekly or monthly, and twenty-one percent said they pray seldom or never. The stats historically have been higher for those who consider themselves born-again, but I theorize that with the digital age and the proliferation of mobile devices and distractions that inherently come with them, the trend is on the decline.

Recently, I read a statistic that the average mobile-connected American is interrupted about every 11 seconds with some form of communication. With all this outside communication, it's no wonder there's less communication going on with the most important person in our lives (God). Most Christians today would agree that there is a need for scheduled (and secluded), consistent prayer (communication) with God.

Most Christians would recognize what many call the Lord's Prayer, found in Matthew 6:5–13. The fact of the matter is that most seminaries label it as the Disciples Example for Prayer. The Lord Jesus laid out the perfect example for us all to follow. Most seminaries would say the actual Lord's Prayer is John 17. Anecdotal, I know, but the main point is that Jesus laid out the perfect example for us on how to pray, and the Christian Vitality Prayer also follows this model.

The Need to Know How to Pray

When I was leading a small group of men and women through a study on prayer, it seemed that the way born-again Christians pray varied in two ways for the most part.

The first is a constant, throughout-the-day acknowledgment of God through communication, such as: "Thank you, God, for my kids," "Thank you, God, for this great parking spot," "Lord, help me get through this," and many others like that. That's awesome. We should have a constant level of communication with our best friend.

The second type of prayer is one that is a regular, focused, and dedicated time of prayer. This is the one that most of them said they do not do often, if at all. Reasons for not doing so varied, but mainly it was that they got out of the habit and had allowed the other priorities and interruptions of life to take over.

The Christian Vitality Prayer is a simple-to-apply solution to this part of your prayer life. The book/program (audios & videos) make it easier to integrate it into your life and should remove many of the obstacles that might hold you back.

I will make the case later in this book for you, but I am confident that when you finish this book, you will be inspired, motivated, equipped, and empowered to make this part of your daily life.

The Need to Know What to Pray

After you've been equipped with the Christian Vitality Prayer (in chapter five), you'll have a great template as to what, how, and when to pray. I will then encourage you to customize and personalize the prayer to fit your individual needs and walk with Christ, but the prayer, as it stands, covers most of your bases. It is described in the following scriptures.

I'd like to highlight several scriptures that to help you know what we are supposed to pray about. By no means are they all-inclusive, but I think you'll find they are great representatives of what we should pray about.

Let us then with confidence draw near to the throne of grace, that we may receive mercy and find grace to help in time of need. Hebrews 4:16 (ESV)

Pray to receive mercy and find grace to help you in times of need, grace being God's "unmerited favor" in your circumstances. He is faithful and will provide.

And so, from the day we heard, we have not ceased to pray for you, asking that you may be filled with the knowledge of his will in all spiritual wisdom and understanding, so as to walk in a manner worthy of the Lord, fully pleasing to him, bearing fruit in every good work and increasing in the knowledge of God. May you be strengthened with all power, according to his glorious might, for all endurance and patience with joy, giving thanks to the Father, who has qualified you to share in the inheritance of the saints in light. Colossians 1:9–12 (ESV)

Pray that you may be filled with the knowledge of his perfect will for your life. In doing so, the promise is that your life will be pleasing to the Lord, will bear fruit, and will increase in the level you know God. Pray also that you may be filled with his power to increase your endurance, patience, and joy. Do so in a manner that is filled with thanks and gratitude, which will lead you to your share of the inheritance of the saints of light.

Trust in him at all times, O people;

   pour out your heart before him;

   God is a refuge for us. Selah Psalm 62:8 (ESV)

But Hannah answered, "No, my lord, I am a woman troubled in spirit. I have drunk neither wine nor strong drink, but I have been pouring out my soul before the Lord. 1 Samuel 1:15 (ESV)

Pour out your heart and soul. This is your loving Father you are dealing with, who is interested in every detail of your life. Lay down everything that is a burden to your heart and soul.

Open my eyes, that I may behold

   wondrous things out of your law.

Give me understanding, that I may keep your law

   and observe it with my whole heart. Psalm 119:18, 34 (ESV)

Pray that God would open your eyes to the opportunities he's provided for you that would bring glory to his Son Jesus and that he would also open your eyes to his perfect will for your life. Pray that he would not only open them, but also give you the understanding needed to help them come to fruition in your life through his word, the Bible.

For this reason I bow my knees before the Father, from whom every family in heaven and on earth is named, that according to the riches of his glory he may grant you to be strengthened with power through his Spirit in your inner being, so that Christ may dwell in your hearts through faith—that you, being rooted and grounded in love, may have strength to comprehend with all the saints what is the breadth and length and height and depth, and to know the love of Christ that surpasses knowledge, that you may be filled with all the fullness of God. Ephesians 3:14–19 (ESV)

Pray for spiritual strength according to his riches in glory with the power of the Holy Spirit so Christ may dwell in your heart through faith, so you would become rooted and grounded in the love of Jesus. Pray that you would retain focus, gain strength with the Holy Spirit, and overcome all obstacles standing in your way to fulfilling God's will for your life. You would comprehend like the saints before us God's all-encompassing love for you through Christ that surpasses knowledge, and you would be filled with all the fullness of God, lacking nothing.

> Therefore, confess your sins to one another and pray for one another, that you may be healed. The prayer of a righteous person has great power as it is working. James 5:16 (ESV)

Last, but definitely not least, confess your sins to one another and pray for one another that you may be healed. Share your struggles and missteps with God in the moment. Receive his forgiveness in the moment, but finish the healing process by sharing them with your family in Christ. When I think of healing, I think of revival, which is a revitalization and strengthening. You can experience a continuous revival in all areas of your life through prayer. We are to pray without ceasing, and in doing so, the revival we experience will also never cease until we go home to heaven.

Chapter 3. Christian Vitality Defined

What Is This New Concept of Christian Vitality?

Well, you've probably heard the term "vital organ" in reference to organs in your body that you could not live without. What about your importance to the body of Christ? Do you feel vitally important to the function of the body of Christ and its fulfillment of God's purposes on earth?

You should! Here's why:

One Body with Many Members

For just as the body is one and has many members, and all the members of the body, though many, are one body, so it is with Christ. For in one Spirit we were all baptized into one body—Jews or Greeks, slaves or free—and all were made to drink of one Spirit.

For the body does not consist of one member but of many. If the foot should say, "Because I am not a hand, I do not belong to the body," that would not make it any less a part of the body. And if the ear should say, "Because I am not an eye, I do not belong to the body," that would not make it any less a part of the body. If the whole body were an eye, where would be the sense of hearing? If the whole body were an ear, where would be the sense of smell? But as it is, God arranged the members in the body, each one of them, as he chose. If all were a single member, where would the body be? As it is, there are many parts, yet one body.

The eye cannot say to the hand, "I have no need of you," nor again the head to the feet, "I have no need of you." On the contrary, the parts of the body that seem to be weaker are indispensable, and on those parts of the body that we think less honorable we bestow the greater honor, and our unpresentable parts are treated with greater modesty, which our more presentable parts do not require. But God has so composed the body, giving greater honor to the part that lacked it, that there may be no division in the body, but that the members may have the same care for one another. If one member suffers, all suffer together; if one member is honored, all rejoice together.

Now you are the body of Christ and individually members of it. And God has appointed in the church first apostles, second prophets, third teachers, then miracles, then gifts of healing, helping, administrating, and various kinds of tongues. Are all apostles? Are all prophets? Are all teachers? Do all work miracles? Do all possess gifts of healing? Do all speak with tongues? Do all interpret? But earnestly desire the higher gifts. And I will show you a still more excellent way. 1 Corinthians 12:12–31 (ESV)

"If one part flourishes, every other part enters into the exuberance." 1 Corinthians 12:26b (The Message)

In Paul's letter to the Corinthians, he makes the point that there really aren't any parts to the body of Christ that are not vital. We all drink from one spirit and are called to fulfill his purposes on earth. We are all vital and working together as one body (if we are all running at full capacity), and we can help God achieve his purposes here on earth in a bigger, better way. If you focus on operating at a higher capacity (flourishing) and "enter into the exuberance" as the The Message translation states, every other part of the Body of Christ will also benefit. What do you think would happen if we all achieved Christian Vitality?

Christian: one who professes belief in the teachings of Jesus Christ

Vitality: a lively or energetic quality; the **power** or ability of something to **continue to live**, be successful, etc.; the **peculiarity distinguishing the living from the nonliving**; capacity to live and develop; also: physical or mental vigor, especially when highly developed**, power of enduring, lively and animated character**[1]

Source: http://www.merriam-webster.com/dictionary/vitality

My end goal is for you is to achieve Christian Vitality as a Christian who distinguishes yourself as one of God's living and not one of the non-living (spiritually dead or not growing). The living are defined as Christians who have experienced a revival in their spiritual, mental, and physical health who help others achieve God's purposes for life—an enduring, flourishing life of loving and serving the Lord and their neighbor at a highly developed capacity.

I desire to help you develop your maturity as a Christian in all areas of your life—a life that is better developed with a higher capacity to live life to the fullest—a life full of the power of God and one that has been physically better developed to endure—a life that would allow God to empower you for a longer period of time in service to him.

My vision for the Christian Vitality Revival Series, of which this is the first book of many to come, is that you will also become a lively and animated Christian who leads life in such a way that you are a light shining brightly as you point toward Jesus as the way for others to live like you. Here's a challenge question from me to you today…

Do you feel you are serving in a way that makes you vital to the body of Christ? If not, please take some steps today toward getting more plugged into how you can serve. Start small if you have to, but get started. Even serving every other Sunday in the first graders' class can make you vital in the life of children learning about the love of Jesus.

I want to also touch on how Christian Vitality is a part of a gradual progression toward your soul's vitality and spiritual vitality. On your quest to bring revival in your prayer life and by affirming God's promises as laid out in the Bible, you will reprogram how your mind thinks and take ownership of truths about yourself. Quite possibly God gave you a dream for your life that has laid dormant—one so big that you currently do not have the capacity to give it much thought. It may internally cause a certain degree of internal conflict. Have you ever thought to yourself, *is* this all that life has for me? No way. I believe if you integrate the Christian Vitality Prayer into your life long term, it will either instill a God-sized dream so BIG for your life that only God can make it come true or God will awaken a dream he gave you long ago.

That is a wonderful thing if you take it into the context that you as a Christian here on Earth have a mission that is spelled out in the Great Commission, but you also have a unique calling in your life. If you allow God to operate fully, he will bring about a revival in not only your life, but the lives of your family, friends, neighborhood, nation, and the world. Your Christian Vitality will have a direct impact on how well you fulfill God's specific mission in spreading the Good News in your unique capacity! Use all of your gifts, talents, skills, life experiences—your everything—to bring about glory to Jesus through your life.

In addition to helping you realize your full potential in Christ and spreading the Good News as an evangelist in your own unique way, I also ask you to help me build momentum in this movement to reach more believers and create more Vital Christians. Helping to spread this message will impact more believers so we can combat and conquer mediocre Christianity and exponentially increase our effectiveness as a global community on the same mission…the Great Commission.

And Jesus came and said to them, "All authority in heaven and on earth has been given to me. Go therefore and make disciples of all nations, baptizing them in the name of the Father and of the Son and of the Holy Spirit, teaching them to observe all that I have commanded you. And behold, I am with you always, to the end of the age." Matthew 28:18–20 (ESV)

So as you run across small challenges that you overcome in your day-to-day life, keep in mind their overall meaning in your pursuit of Christian Vitality. The small victories along the way will build you up into a Christian who will (God willing) have a greater capacity for survival or for the continuation of a meaningful or purposeful existence. You'll be increasing the effectiveness of your service to the Lord Jesus and continuing to live under his full measure of blessing down here.

To some extent, Christian Vitality is the goal we are keeping our eyes on every day as we pile on small victories for Jesus in all areas of our lives…and our spiritual growth and service to the Lord. Victories in Progress we are, you and I! Victories…

Modern research scientists are discovering new breakthroughs every day that can accelerate the attainment of good health and help make this a reality for everyone. I've pieced together all the best techniques, tips, and strategies into the Christian Vitality Revival Series of books and programs to help you transform your spiritual, mental, and physical health to higher levels.

In all of the Revival Series books, you will be encouraged to bless yourself with some quiet Jesus Time. The Christian Vitality Prayer is not only a great solution to help do that, but it can also be customized or expanded to make a very personal, intimate prayer between you and your best friend. At the same time, you will use modern scientific principles to help make them effective and have a greater impact on your soul (your mind, your will, and your emotions), restoring and reviving any damage caused in your life up to now that may be holding you back.

Throughout this program, you'll be applying timely, devotional-style Biblical Wisdom to teach and inspire you to achieve the next level in your walk with Christ.

Modern scientific discoveries are also revealed that will help you cheat (or hack) your soul in a way to get a larger return on your investment of time, energy, and money to achieve the maximum results.

I will also be sharing with you personal revelations that I've garnered through years of prayer and meditation on God's word through the Christian Vitality Prayer and my SOAPP technique to help you Encounter God Every Day!

You'll be joining me and thousands of other sisters and brothers. Essentially, we'll all be going through the program together on a daily basis, morning and night.

I'm excited for us. From this day forward I want you to consider yourself a Victory in Progress. That's right! A VIP in the community of believers striving toward the upward call of God in Christ Jesus! Let's do this together, shall we?

The Christian Vitality Lifestyle

A Christian Vitality Lifestyle is a committed, surrendered, and empowered life lived fully in the present moment.

Commit and Surrender to God's Vision for Your Life!

Committing our lives to the Lord means a constant surrender of our ideas, plans, and choices. It means dying to ourselves in every area of our lives so that God can shine through them. We must abstain from the desires of this world so we can hear his still, small voice and be directed towards his will for our lives.

As Christians, we should desire to make a significant impact on the world for Jesus. We cannot do this on our own. We need his help, and Jesus sent the Holy Spirit just for this very purpose. You need to lean on him for every choice you make along the way. By utilizing the Christian Vitality Prayer, you can affirm that you retain focus on your God-inspired goals, gain strength to achieve them, and overcome all obstacles with the help of the Holy Spirit in addition to the many other gifts of the Spirit.

Our dreams (or visions for our lives) need to be bigger than ourselves and what we can do on our own. We ought to want God to use our day-to-day activities in ways beyond what we would or could do on our own. This is not a solo journey, but one in which we are cooperating with God and operating together as a team.

I've heard it once said that "Every Christian should have a dream so big it takes God himself to fulfill it." For that to happen, we must ask God for a God-sized vision (dream) for our lives. That vision will include not only your individual mission here on earth but also God's vision for your spiritual, mental, and physical health.

If you haven't done so recently or you find yourself at a place in your life where you feel you've lost sight of God's vision for your life, I invite you to take the time now away from this book and go into prayer to ask God to grant or restore His vision for your life. Ask him to reveal to you **the vision he has for you that would lead you down a path to serve the Lord with all your heart, all your soul (mind, will, and emotions), and all your body.**

You need to understand--there is nothing you can do yourself to make this happen. This vision or dream for your life can only come from the hand of God.

Come back to this book only after you've taken the time to commune with God about his vision for your life.

Taking Responsibility

Responsibility can be broken down into its core meaning of the ability to respond and the ability to make a choice. It can also mean taking personal ownership.

You might remember that in the preface to this book, I referred to you as the hero of this journey we are embarking on together. You absolutely are a hero whose victory is in progress.

The only catch is that you are a hero who has been called on this journey in your current world and your existing state of health and circumstances. You are called to a new world of health and happiness in your future.

It's a safe assumption that since you've read this far, you are, for the moment, accepting the Lord's call on your life to make a change, to do things differently going forward, and to build a life in pursuit of glory for Jesus Christ in every aspect of your life—a new, completely Christ-centered world.

One thing we must do before we carry on is address the fact that your current state of health (spiritual, mental, and physical) is not where you want it to be. It's a product of all the life choices you've made up to this point. I firmly believe that our lives are the product of all the cumulative choices we make along the way. The only way to change our current state of affairs is to start accumulating better choices. We are (or will become) what we repeatedly do.

We still need to take responsibility and ownership for where we are right now however. You can have a dialog with God that sounds something like this: *"Yes, Lord, my health is not what it could be or will be, and I accept the fact that I've made some poor choices to get to where I am today. Please, Lord, help guide me in my steps as I pursue a better life for myself—one that glorifies you in all ways. AMEN!"*

No, it's not all your fault, but it is all your responsibility. You've been taught by your well-meaning parents to live certain ways. You've been lied to by family, friends, acquaintances, advertisers, and even government officials over the years. All of it was likely based on information that, at the time, was the best information they had. Nevertheless, it made an impression on your soul and your belief systems.

What can be learned can also be unlearned, though. Kids are not typically programmed for success, and neither are adults for that matter. Making decisions based on old information or training has to stop from this point forward because you personally have unlimited access to up-to-date information backed by scientific research through the Internet. There are no more valid excuses from now on.

Take the ownership of how things are, but also commit to yourself to be a life-long learner. Always strive to make yourself aware of the current science and biblical wisdom that may affect your health, and implement it into your life. That last part is the most critical. Knowing the information without doing something with it is all on you and will make the difference between you living a healthy, happy life and missing it by a mile.

So whoever knows the right thing to do and fails to do it, for him it is sin. James 4:17(ESV)

When taking James 4:17 literally and applying it to all aspects of your life, it's not much of a stretch to say not applying the knowledge in this book (and what you find on the Internet) that could do you good is a sin. With knowledge comes great responsibility, though. Luke 12:48 also tells us that "to whom much is given, of him much will be required, and from him to whom they entrusted much, they will demand the more." This expands more on our responsibility when given actionable information. God will honor you when you honor him with the obedient choices you make once you know better.

I'll strive to do my very best here and throughout the entire Christian Vitality Revival Series to give you as much actionable information as possible, but the truth be told, this book will be a work in progress that is constantly updated as new information and discoveries become available. To make certain you are up-to-date on the latest information, you can subscribe to our blog or newsletter at http://christianvitality.com. I'll share our latest discoveries with you as they surface.

No one who is good at making excuses is good at taking care of their lives. Stop making excuses to not do the right thing, and start looking for reasons why you should take action toward them now.

Self-love vs. Self-loathe

A challenge we all face at times is the struggle with self-loathing. I want to address that now as we've just finished acknowledging and taking responsibility for our current state of affairs. Something I heard in my very early twenties that has stuck with me my whole life is this:

God made YOU, Christ saved YOU, and that makes YOU a person of tremendous worth! – Author Unknown

We go throughout our Christian lives trying to learn how to die to self, which I am a major proponent of. Some might even say that as we mature as Christians, we even develop an element of self-loathing because we despise at times the things we say or do when we allow ourselves to operate in that self-centered capacity. The issue at hand, however, is that we can never escape ourselves. We may label it as our sinful nature that we are inherently born with, but the fact of the matter is that God made you just the way you are. You need to accept that you are a gift God has granted to this world to bring him glory with your life. Even though we've stumbled along the way, made bad choices, and sinned, God can use those life-long experiences to bring himself glory if we will let him. Our "self" or sinful nature does not have to get in our way toward the pursuit of a better life.

Christ saved you on the cross and shed his blood to atone for you and so that you could be sanctified (set a part for him) for his glory here on earth. You are a new creation in Christ and can be made new in his image. It's not a once and done process though. It is a continual process where we can be made new today, in this very moment, as we obediently accept his call on our lives and make choices that glorify him.

You are tremendously worthy only because he is worthy. He lives inside of you the moment you receive Christ's salvation. You became one of God's children, and as 1 John 4:4 (ESV) says, "Little children, you are from God and have overcome them, for he who is in you is greater than he who is in the world." We just have to live like it daily, moment by moment, surrendered to God and his will for our lives. So you are never allowed to get down on yourself, or as some like to call it "hating on yourself," because you would, in a sense, discount everything Jesus did for you on the cross.

Instead, I'd like to propose that you make it a lifelong habit to love yourself and accept who you are in the moment, keeping in mind that the next choice you make can bring glory to God. Practice self-forgiveness and confession of sin in the moment with God. You can apply James 5:16 (ESV) in the moment, where he says to "confess your sins to one another and pray for one another, that you may be healed. The prayer of a righteous person has great power as it is working." You can move on and confess to the Lord that you let him down, and you'll do your very best for him on your next opportunity to choose. Receive his forgiveness in real time, and then put it behind you. Move on toward the upward call of God. You'll be affirming these same truths from the Christian Vitality Prayer and making them part of your soul: "All my debts have long since been paid for and forgiven by the blood of Jesus Christ, and I honor him by forgetting them and learning from them." Honor Jesus by receiving forgiveness for your sins in the moment, and move on.

Origins of the Christian Vitality Prayer

There was a time in my life when I spent about 30–50% of my life traveling for a living. I was a regional sales manager for a high tech company in the electrical and electronics industry. What I did for work is not what matters, it's what I did during all that down time on the plane at thirty-three thousand feet and in airports and hotel rooms.

I spent those five years diving into every self-help and success book I could find. I also spent that time reading the entire Bible five times (the New Testament ten times) and really getting to know the character of God and how he shapes how humans succeed in life. I'll admit a lot of the authors of books I've read are secular (many are also strong Christians), but what I found to be true after all that research and study is a universal truth:

There's a Universal Conspiracy for or Against Your Individual Success—You Decide!

You see, I believe God's greatest expression of his love for humanity is allowing us a free will. We have a free will to choose--to choose him; to choose an abundant life or a life of lack, to choose his plan for our lives or the plan of the enemy, to follow the teachings of Jesus Christ or follow the ways of the world. If we choose God's plan, I think we can count on the promise of Romans 8:26–28:

Meanwhile, the moment we get tired in the waiting, God's Spirit is right alongside helping us along. If we don't know how or what to pray, it doesn't matter. He does our praying in and for us, making prayer out of our wordless sighs, our aching groans. He knows us far better than we know ourselves, knows our pregnant condition, and keeps us present before God. That's why we can be so sure that every detail in our lives of love for God is worked into something good. (The Message)

Putting it a different way, you get to decide whether you have a successful life or an unsuccessful one…a happy one or an unhappy one. Either way you choose, you are choosing what kind of life you're going to have, and you'll get it.

Once you decide and commit (submit) your plans (long-term and short-term) for your life to God and have his blessing, you will succeed (Proverbs 16:3 Pastor Dan Translation).

Whatever you do, do it as service to him, and he will guarantee your success. Proverbs 16:3 (The Voice)

Commit your work to the Lord, and your plans will be established. Proverbs 16:3 (ESV)

Another byproduct (or extreme blessing to me and hopefully to you too) of that time of self-reflection, biblical study and science of human success study is a prayer with some affirmations built into it that I've prayed for literally the last ten years straight. Some days it's first thing in the morning and then again at night. Sometimes it's a portion of the prayer to remind me of God's promises throughout the day. Sometimes it's a portion right before I jump on the weight scale or after an apparent problem in my life.

This prayer helped birth many of the strategies that are used in the Christian Vitality Life Revival Programs, like Real-time Living, Soul Conditioning, and the 40-day Christian Weight Loss Program. You'll find the entire programs that I've built have this prayer at their foundations.

This evening when you have time (and if you're game, do it every day), please pray the Christian Vitality Prayer with me. Own it. If you can commit to memorizing it and praying it every morning and/or evening before you go to bed, I faithfully and firmly believe that **God will use it to change your life on the inside and outside**. It will likely help you believe different things about yourself, which will lead you to achieving abundant success in all areas of your life. It will touch areas of your life that you could not have ever imagined.

My hope is that this prayer God helped me craft is a blessing to you and helps bring healing and revival to your spirit, soul, and body. The result will be a closer walk with the Lord Jesus and a healthier, happier you who has a longer stay here on earth. In Jesus' name, AMEN!

Introduction to the Christian Vitality Prayer

The Christian Vitality Prayer takes only two minutes of your time, twice a day, and it will completely change your life. You're worth it for the price paid for your life. So please put all distractions aside and divert all of your attention to this entire training. The entire training program takes less time to complete than sitting through a meal. You'll likely want to go through it a couple of times as I believe the content God revealed to me is rich with his wisdom and will be a blessing to you.

Due to the science behind this program's design, this prayer will reprogram your subconscious and conscious mind. I know it sounds weird to combine your mind and psychology when we speak about something that is so "spiritual" like prayer, right? It's okay to think I'm weird. I love you anyway; just don't give up on me yet. Please hear me out to the end, and even after you do, I beg you to please try it out for yourself. The first few times you may even feel silly, and some of the prayer you may not even completely believe to be true yet. That's okay. It's all Bible-based truth, and the fact of the matter is it just flat out works.

That's what you wanted after all, isn't it? **A system or strategy to integrate prayer into your life in a life-changing way?** This is it! Or at least one of them that I've discovered and am sharing with you now.

Well, my goal for this training is that it is received as something beautifully inspiring. I hope you will not only go through this training and get warm fuzzies and an uplift in your prayer life (and life overall) for the moment but that you will also take action on this material today and integrate it into your life long term. My goal is to help YOU produce a life change in and for you--one that would allow you to increase your level of maturity in Christ and increase your level of Christian Vitality and abundance.

When you use and affirm the Christian Vitality Prayer that I will reveal to you, it will start to change your thoughts about yourself and God. Once your thoughts change, you will then start to change your beliefs (beliefs deeply rooted in your soul). Once your beliefs have taken root, you will start to change your expectations for life. Once your expectations have changed, you will start to change your actions (take different ones than you've ever taken before). And once your actions have changed, you will revolutionize your life by changing your outcomes. Everything in your life will start to align with God's will for your life, and I believe you'll become a spiritually, mentally, and physically healthier and happier believer. You will be more in-step with God and what he wants for your life.

You might have noticed that I emphasized beliefs taking root in your soul. That's very important and part of why this prayer and the manner I suggest you use it are so effective at producing a tremendous, positive change in the people's lives who use it.

You see, the Christian Vitality Prayer is one tool in a toolbox for Christians I am building called Soul Conditioning™. I know what you're saying. *Okay, Pastor, you are getting weird on me again.* Hold on a minute. Please let me explain a little more….

Many pastors before me have taught, and it is accepted knowledge in Christian circles, even those in seminaries, that your soul consists of three parts: your mind, your will, and your emotions. They make you completely and uniquely you. It's a big part of your identity as a human. You may or may not have complete control over any one of them at any given time, but what is true is that God gave us the ability to control them. And that, my friend, is critical for you to understand because it is the secret to making a purposeful and significant change in any area of your life. It doesn't matter if you want to lose a few pounds, learn how to increase your confidence in life, excel at your job, or even get great at meeting new people. Whatever the life skill or life change you want, your soul can be a friend or foe. Most often in regards to creating a positive change in our lives, our soul is what holds us back.

There's a bit of confusion when it comes to soul versus spirit. When we were saved, we received Christ's salvation by confessing with our mouths and believing in our hearts that Jesus Christ is the son of God and rose from the grave. Done. You are saved. You are also granted the new privilege as one of God's children with your name written in the Book of Life as one who has access to the fruit of the Holy Spirit, such as: love, joy, peace, forbearance, kindness, goodness, faithfulness, gentleness, and self-control (Galatians 5:22–23).

The Holy Spirit has many names given him to describe what he does, like counselor, comforter, etc. You have access to many gifts of the Holy Spirit that can be of HUGE benefit to you in your service to the Lord. All are meant for one purpose: to bring glory to the Son of God. They can also grant us power over our soul, which is, again, our minds, wills, and emotions. I don't want to take away the spotlight from the gifts of the Holy Spirit as I believe they are tools just as powerful as any that man has discovered with modern science.

That said, let me say that I believe the function of science in general is to describe and discover how things work through observation and testing. Basically, science is just man's way to describe how God created the universe (which includes us, by the way).

By applying modern scientific discoveries about how our minds, wills, and emotions can be affected by using strategies tested by research doctors from Harvard, Yale, Princeton, and many others, Soul Conditioning™ is simply using what works to effect a change in human behavior to help accelerate personal development in human beings. So to some extent, I've taken biblical wisdom and modern science and come up with tools to create positive changes in Christians. The Christian Vitality Prayer is just one of those in an ever expanding toolbox of Soul Conditioning. Stay tuned for a future release of the Soul Conditioning book and an online training program like this one.

You might be wondering, "*How could this actually change my mind, will, and emotions?*" I'm glad you asked, sister or brother.

Without going into too much of the science behind it, I just need to have you live a little by faith here. What scientists have discovered is that by saying affirmations (the Christian Vitality Prayer is full of Bible-based promises that we affirm for our lives) the first thing in the morning and the last thing before we fall asleep, when our subconscious mind is most open to suggestions, our subconscious mind accepts whatever we plant in it. Whether it is good or evil, it doesn't have the luxury of logic like our conscious minds do. So in another weird way, by doing affirmations and the Christian Vitality Prayer first thing in the morning and last thing at night, we are reprogramming our subconscious minds to believe the biblical promises that we affirm. I know this is a little light on the subject, but I have a whole library full of books that are written solely on this topic. I will give you a list of references at the end of this book if you want to learn more. Just trust me on this. Or at the very least, try it and watch the magic happen in your life. The mechanism of how this works is what I mentioned before, but it is worth mentioning again:

When you use and affirm the Christian Vitality Prayer that I will reveal to you later (in chapter five), it will start to change your thoughts. Some of the bad ones planted by your past will be uprooted and replaced with good ones, and your thoughts will then start to change your beliefs. Your beliefs will start to change your expectations (and essentially change your level of faith to some degree), your expectations will change your actions, and your actions then will change your outcomes.

Everything in your life will start to align with God's will for your life (as promised in the Bible), and I believe you'll become a spiritually, mentally, and physically healthier and happier believer. You will be light-years closer to fulfilling your identity as a mature believer in Jesus Christ.

God is the great I am, the Creator and Sustainer of the whole universe. That's his role. That is his identity.

I believe you can gain great clarity in your life if you strive to achieve your full and complete identity in Christ. That is your role.

You are saved by his grace and are called to his purposes on earth. But what is your unique identity in Christ? Are you fulfilling your destiny? Do you have a God-inspired dream for your life that is so big that only God can fulfill it? I believe that every Christian should have a God-sized dream for their life—one so BIG that it will take God to bring it to fruition. It will only happen, however, if we will cooperate with him and grow fully mature as Paul writes in Colossians 1:28. Jesus is the one I proclaim, much like Paul does, admonishing and teaching everyone with all wisdom, so that I may present everyone fully mature in Christ.

Are you fully mature in Christ? If not, why not?

Do you want to join me in your journey?

God gave us the ability to choose with our free will. So choose the change today and put the Christian Vitality Prayer into practice right now. If not now, when?

May the Lord Jesus bless you richly and abundantly on your journey to fulfill God's perfect will for YOUR life. In Jesus' name, AMEN!

Chapter 4. Answering Some Possible Objections to Using the Christian Vitality Prayer

I'm going to make a statement that will likely shock you, but stay with me. I'll explain what I mean afterwards, and I think once I do, you'll likely agree with me too.

"I hate Religion, and I believe God does too."

What do I mean by that? I define Religion as man's rules applied to the heart of God's original intention for man. The reason I hate Religion is that man, by his very nature, with all his inherent faults, often builds a religion by applying God-inspired rituals to his life to help him remember God's laws and intentions for him. Man then places so much focus and thought and energy into the religion that he finds himself forgetting the original heart of God for himself. Many of the Christian denominations to some extent could arguably be guilty of that. And to some extent, when Religion does this, it creates sin (separation) in our lives. Sin, after all, separates us from God. God hates sin because it is the very antithesis of his nature. So our sinful nature is often at odds with God's nature.

Here is a reference for why God hates sin:
http://www.gotquestions.org/God-hate-sin.html

So I share with you today the Christian Vitality Prayer, and I want to preface this discussion with the fact that I am not proposing you make this prayer your religion. It is my personal ritual borne from many years of prayer, meditation, and study of God's word and of many of the best secular self-help books on the planet. Arguably, many of these self-help books and gurus have discovered truths about man that are effective at producing very positive change in human beings. I firmly believe that if a pastor or seminary student or even an everyday Christian were to delve deeper into why any of the secular self-help programs work, they would discover that biblical wisdom is at the heart of it all. Would you agree? They work because they can be substantiated by God's Living Word, the Bible.

So I challenge you to accept this prayer as my gift to you and accept it at face value as an imperfect creation of man (me) that is presented with a grateful heart to God for revealing these many things to me. Check it all out for yourself against the Bible and the Holy Spirit's counsel before you make it your own. Use it as it stands now, or modify it based on the Bible and what the Holy Spirit reveals to you in your own prayer life. Please try it out for yourself, though, as it stands now for a while (maybe a week or two) and see how it affects your life. I firmly believe it will be a tremendous blessing to anyone who does.

You and possibly the many pastors out there may be thinking to yourself, *Is this just another Jabez prayer?* And I would say absolutely not, although I think many believers may start down that path with this as I plan to make it public as an introduction to the Christian Vitality way of thinking and living. Portions of the prayer are a prosperity and abundance prayer, but the heart of it is that of John 10:10 (The Message) when Jesus said, "I came so they can have real and eternal life, more and better life than they ever dreamed of." That is the heart behind those portions of the prayer. The intention is not to teach believers how to manipulate God to bring them wealth and riches, although it may and likely will have a material impact on your life. The intention is to build and grow your faith while speaking to your conscious and subconscious mind to help reverse some of the damage that may have been caused over the course of your life—damage that is hindering God's full measure of abundance in your life. A more abundant and better life than you ever dreamed of.

I will go over the prayer in detail and reveal the entire prayer to you, but I believe there are a couple of clarifications that need to be addressed as they could be mistakenly taken out of context and my original heart of the prayer.

The first of these is the use of the word universe. It may not resonate with some and may even sound a little new age. I challenge anyone to find in the Bible where it contradicts that our Creator is not God of the entire universe. The intention is not to be new age; my heart is to give God credit for it all—the ENTIRE universe. He is the King, after all, of EVERYTHING.

The second sticking point in the prayer for some of you could be when it refers to, "I deserve, desire, and willingly receive the abundance and prosperity of the universe. It flows to me and is promised to me." This sounds super selfish, self-centered, and worldly, doesn't it? Well, the heart behind this can be summed up in a few thoughts. John 10:10, as we discussed earlier, covers the abundance Jesus himself wants you to have—an abundant life, more abundant than you've ever dreamed.

You are also a child of God and had your name written in the Book of Life on the day of your salvation. You're now an ambassador of Christ. You've been commissioned to achieve God's will on earth, and God wants to equip you abundantly to achieve his purpose and will for your life.

Abundance isn't all about money and wealth, and wealth is not always money and material things. God's word is a wealth of wisdom and knowledge, and the book of Proverbs refers to wealth and riches being promised to the one who possesses Wisdom.

A third, and probably the biggest, internal check you might have in the prayer would be where it says "and is mine to keep." The word "keep" is not meant in the sense that it is all yours to keep for yourself. "Mine, mine, mine" might be a bell that rings in your head when you go through the prayer and hit that portion of it. The word "keep" in the prayer is equivalent to the word "steward." You are a steward of God's wealth in your life. And a good steward is constantly waiting on the Lord (like a waiter waits on tables) and asking God what he should do with what God has blessed him with. "Those who wait on the Lord shall renew their strength" actually refers to that kind of waiting…not the kind of waiting that you do in a line at a movie. Waiting actually means serving, tending to, and taking care to meet the needs and demands of. So the word "keep" in the Christian Vitality Prayer means steward, not keep for myself or own.

With all that said, I'm certain you may come up with other objections or reasons not to use the Christian Vitality Prayer. If any are of particular concern, I would ask that you join us all on the Facebook page dedicated to the book. I'm there with the rest of the community of believers who are on this journey together.

Rather than come up with reasons not to use it, focus on all the reasons you should try it. What do you have to lose? I am certain your life will never be the same if you give it a shot. If that's not enough, I double-dog-dare you to try it.

Chapter 5. The Christian Vitality Prayer

The following section is a full transcript of the Christian Vitality Prayer MP3. The actual Prayer is only the blue-highlighted text. Make sure to visit our website for a free copy of the MP3 that you can use in your own prayer time.

MP3 Content Starts Here

For a FREE Copy Visit: ChristianVitality.com/Free-Bonuses

Password at the website is = revival

"Here's what I want you to do: find a quiet, secluded place so you won't be tempted to role-play before God. Just be there as simply and honestly as you can manage. The focus will shift from you to God, and you will begin to sense his grace. This is your Father you are dealing with, and he knows better than you what you need. With a God like this loving you, you can pray very simply like this:" Matthew 6:6–13 (The Message)

God made YOU! Christ saved you! And that makes you a person of tremendous worth to him. Treat yourself with this quiet time away from life, and have some Jesus Time right here, right now. Be 100% present when you pray this prayer with me.

Put the thoughts of everything else out of your mind, and just think of this moment…this special moment you're going to have with God…and kneel if you like or stand…close your eyes if you like, and raise your hands toward heaven…arms stretched wide like you're asking God to notice you.

Oh God, Creator and Sustainer of the whole universe. You are my loving Father and interested in every detail of my life. You only have good for me and desire to give me healing, wholeness, and forgiveness. Therefore, I place myself at your feet, under your authority, and your control, and protection for your will to be done in my life.

Everything over which you've given me authority, Lord, I place at your feet: my family (name them), my loved ones (name them), my blessings (name them), my gifts, my talents, and my life experiences. Everything, Lord, over which you've given me authority Lord I place at your feet right now….

[I often do this kneeling and physically act out laying things at his feet.]

Now picture their faces….

Do you have any burdens right now? Lay them down at his feet.

Do you have any praises to thank him for? Let yourself feel the gratitude…feel it…be grateful. Thank God for all he's done for you.

In Christ, I deserve, desire, and willingly receive the abundance and prosperity of the universe. It flows to me, is promised to me, and is mine to keep. In return for my obedience to the Lord by fully utilizing the gifts he has given me, the universe benefits directly and indirectly by the value added by my obedient actions and prosperity.

All my debts have long since been paid for and forgiven by the blood of Jesus Christ, and I honor the Lord by forgetting them and learning from them.

Think about that…all your debts have been forgiven. Now receive that forgiveness and own it. Honor him by receiving it.

I retain focus and gain strength with help from the Holy Spirit and overcome ALL obstacles.

For yours is the Kingdom, the Power, and Glory forever and ever. AMEN!

Now go out into the rest of this day and claim your newfound FREEDOM…freedom to do your VERY best for the Lord and receive all that he has for you.

Remember, he is your source and supply, and all your needs are met…take that belief into every circumstance today, and you'll have Christian Vitality. Every circumstance…

MP3 Content Ends Here

For a FREE Copy Visit: ChristianVitality.com/Free-Bonuses

Password at the website is = revival

Chapter 6. How to Stop Worrying the Christian Way

The answer is Real-time Living and the Christian Vitality Prayer.

Real-time Living

Jesus is the Great I AM, not I was or I will be. It's the greatest of all names for the Lord Jesus. We hear it often sung in songs and come across it in scripture, but I think it is important to point out that Jesus Christ our Lord is the one and the same God whom Moses spoke of when he had the encounter at the burning bush.

God told Moses his name is "I AM THAT I AM." The Hebrew variation on that name is YAHWEH or JEHOVAH. Jesus has been given all authority on earth, heaven, and under the earth. He is the one true God, not one of many gods, but the one and only (Acts 4:12; 1 Timothy. 2:5; 1 Corinthians. 8:4) and even references himself as: "I am he [God]," (when he is responding to the Samaritan woman at the well). "Before Abraham was born, I am," (John 8:58). "I am," (John 4:26, 6:20, 8:24, 8:28, 8:58; 13:19; 18:5). "I am the Bread of Life," (John 6:35). "I am the Light of the World," (John 8:12); "I am the Door," (John 10:7,9). "I am the Good Shepherd," (John 10:11,14). "I am the Resurrection and Life," (John 11:25-26). "I am the way, the truth, and the life," (John 14:6). "I am the True Vine," (John 15:1, 5). Finally, "'I am the Alpha and the

Omega,' says the Lord God, 'who is and who was and who is to come, the Almighty,'" (Revelation. 1:8).

Jesus is the Lord of the present, the past, and the future. There is no doubt about that. I think, however, that we humans are locked here in the present. We cannot, and should not try to, live in the past or the future. That is a revelation I feel I was given recently in reading the "Sermon on the Mount."

I believe we are all called to live what I call real-time living, which is living in the moment and forgetting about the past and the future. I don't mean to give up on future planning or taking short trips into the future as directed by a vision God grants us for our lives. I'm talking about day-to-day living and living solely in the moment.

Visit the future for brief periods of time if, and only if, you are accompanied by God himself to show you what he has planned for you. **Go into the future with a great deal of prayer and meditation on his word in deep surrender to his will for your life, knowing that he always has your best interest in mind. He has, after all, the master plan for the universe and knows where you fit into it perfectly**—just as the Christian Vitality Prayer is modeled.

Think about what you know about Jesus and how he lived his daily life. The Bible reveals to us quite a bit about how Jesus lived while he was here on earth. If you go over the Bible passages, I think you'll find that Jesus lived his life moment by moment while asking God for direction every step of the way. I know and agree with you that yes, Jesus did know his future as was prophesied about him in the scriptures, but I think he lived every moment of his life in real time.

When confiding in God, Jesus would often sneak away to pray. In times of prayer, he would commune with God the Father to get fresh revelation for his life. So take God with you when you are looking to get fresh revelation about your future. Obtain vision for your life about the future cooperatively with God. Never take a trip into the future without taking God with you. Then come back to the present and make your choices for the now in such a way as to be congruent with God's vision for your life in the moment.

Paul tells us in his letter to the Philippians that we should be "forgetting what lies behind and straining forward to what lies ahead." I think many of us have trouble with this, and this is critical for achieving Christian Vitality. You must forget the past. Don't spend any time there. You've received forgiveness for your past transgressions, and it's time to put them to rest. I believe the only value the past has for us in the present is for us to use it to make sure we don't make the same mistakes again. If we dwell on the past, we are not living in the present. It's like driving a car with your eyes on the rear-view mirror all the time. You wouldn't do that, would you? That would be dangerous as you might run into something. The same is true about your past. Put it behind you for good, my friend.

Paul also stated in Philippians 3:13 that we are to strain forward to what lies ahead. You have a bright future in Christ, and God has some really cool things planned for your future. But I think many Christians (myself included) have a tendency to worry about things that "might happen" in the future. Now, that is where we get it wrong. A term I learned from my lovely wife Diana long ago is "future tripping." This is taking a life circumstance or event and projecting what it might mean into the future. What could happen? What does this mean to my future? We let our crazy, often negative minds run with it, and before we know it, our lives as we know them are going to end. That's just not right. Instead, we should put Paul's advice from Philippians 4:6–9 into practice.

Don't fret or worry. Instead of worrying, pray. Let petitions and praises shape your worries into prayers, letting God know your concerns. Before you know it, a sense of God's wholeness, everything coming together for good, will come and settle you down. It's wonderful what happens when Christ displaces worry at the center of your life.

Summing it all up, friends, I'd say you'll do best by filling your minds and meditating on things true, noble, reputable, authentic, compelling, gracious—the best, not the worst; the beautiful, not the ugly; things to praise, not things to curse. Put into practice what you learned from me, what you heard and saw and realized. Do that, and God, who makes everything work together, will work you into his most excellent harmonies. Philippians 4:6–9 (The Message)

Why should we focus all of our attention on the present and nothing else? Well, the Lord Jesus commanded it in his sermon on the mount (Matthew 6:34, The Message) when he said, "Give your entire attention to what God is doing right now, and don't get worked up about what may or may not happen tomorrow. God will help you deal with whatever hard things come up when the time comes." See, we are to live in the now. Be real-time Christians serving the Lord and living how he did when he was here. In the moment, ask God, "What's next, Papa? What can I do now, Lord, in this moment to bring you glory with my life, this decision, right now?" And when you do ask, be direct with God. Jesus told us a bit later in that same sermon (Matthew 7:7–11, The Message), "Don't bargain with God. Be direct. Ask for what you need…don't you think the God who conceived you in love will be even better [than how you would provide for your kids]?"

In the English language and specifically in America, the word gift and present are synonymous. At Christmas and other holidays we give presents. Well, you may have heard or seen the expression that "today is a gift, that's why they call it the present."

"Yesterday is history, tomorrow is a mystery, today is a gift, that's why they call it the present! Also, remember that it isn't the size of the gift that matters, but the size of the heart that gives it." – Ellen Glasgow

Appreciate God's generous gift (the present) of today. Make an effort to build "magic moments" (as Tony Robbins calls them) throughout the day where you truly help yourself feel a deep sense of gratitude and appreciation for the little things. Be in the moment. Be present. Be grateful. Show God how much you appreciate his huge, giving heart for the gift of the present moment. Like The Message says in Philippians 4:4a, "Celebrate God all day, every day. I mean, revel in Him!"

At the end of our lives, we are not going to remember all the chaos, challenges, or frustrations that we experienced down here. We'll go back to "magic moments" we had while we were down here. So make certain that you take as many as you can with you.

What would it be like if you woke up five years, ten years, or even twenty years from now and realized you could not remember any of it? That precious time would be lost completely. Doesn't even the thought of that possibility concern you? I've heard many people throughout the years and history talk about how life flew by. How they don't even remember portions of their lives. "Where did it all go?" is what they ask themselves.

I think we should make a conscious effort to ensure that doesn't happen, and I think the secret to doing so is living in the moment, in the now, by being 100% present as often as possible.

So the next time you are with a friend, a family member, or even alone with the Lord, make absolutely certain you are present. You are here, right now. You can do that by turning off or blocking your thoughts of the past or future and filling yourself with a deep sense of gratitude and appreciation for the present moment. Also, be sure to block out or turn off any distractions that you may have like cellular phones, computers, TVs, etc.

Finally, as part of a Christian Vitality Lifestyle, you must live your life in real time as Jesus did. Work these words of scripture into your life that are not incidental additions to your life but foundational words. They are words to build a Vital Christian's life on. He warned us in Matthew 7:26–27 that if we only use his words in Bible studies and don't work them into our lives, we are like a "foolish man" whose home washed away with the storms of life. When he concluded that wonderful sermon, the crowd listening burst into applause because they never heard anyone teach like that. The Message says in Matthew 7:29 that "It was apparent that he was living everything he was saying—quite a contrast to their religion teachers! This was the best teaching they had ever heard."

Thank you, God, that someone was around to write all of this down so that we know how to live our lives just like Jesus did.

So when you are taking Jesus Time and using the Christian Vitality Prayer, keep in mind how Jesus lived his life, and surrender yourself to the present moment with God. If there are worries or burdens you are carrying around with you about your future, lay them down at his feet, and take a trip into the future with Jesus by your side, owning the promises he has for you. He is, after all, your source and supply and interested in EVERY detail of YOUR life. He's in control of your universe.

Doesn't the thought of this bring you peace and freedom? "Before you know it, a sense of God's wholeness, everything coming together for good, will come and settle you down. It's wonderful what happens when Christ displaces worry at the center of your life." Philippians 4:7 (The Message)

Chapter 7. Start Your Prayer-Powered Life Revival Today

God is the great I am as we went over in the last chapter. That is his identity—the Creator and Sustainer of the whole universe, who is interested in every detail of your life.

I pray that my deep-rooted conviction and belief has come through to you. What I believe to be a fact-- you will gain great clarity in your life when you strive to achieve your full and complete identity in Christ.

You know you are saved by his grace and are called to his purposes in your life on earth. But what is your unique Identity in Christ? Are you fulfilling your destiny? Do you have a God-inspired dream for your life so big that only God can fulfill it?

Like I said before, but I think deserves repeating is that I believe that YOU should have a God-sized dream for your life…one so BIG that it will take God to bring it to reality in your life. It will only happen, however, if you will co-operate with him and grow fully mature as Paul wrote to the Colossians (Colossians 1:28). So that I may present everyone fully mature in Christ.

Are you fully mature in Christ? If not, why not? Do you think applying the Christian Vitality Prayer could have a significant impact on how you see your identity in Christ?

God gave you the ability to choose with your free will.

I implore you to choose this change in your life today, right now. If not now, when?

If I could speak with you face to face, I would beg you to give this a shot.

Please use any or all of the tools that are laid out for you here and the additional resources I have provided to make integrating this into your life easy.

In addition to this book, you can use the prayer PDF (you can print it out) to memorize and customize the prayer and make it your own.

There's the professionally mastered MP3 file that I had created for you to use on your phone, tablet, or other device.

There's even a video of all of this available with some additional resources.

I tried to make it as easy as possible for you. Please do me the honor of using it. **I sincerely believe it will start a revival in your life in all areas. That in turn will instill and awaken a God-sized dream for your life, which will most likely lead to a revival in your ministry and service to Christ.**

Feel free to reach out to me and share your success or struggles. I will do my very best to help you achieve the revival you know you want deep down in your soul.

Links to the extra FREE resources included in your purchase are in the next section.

How To Start Your Prayer Powered Life Revival Today

Step 1) Click Here -> ChristianVitality.com/Free-Bonuses (PASSWORD=revival)

Step 2) Watch the short getting started video.

Step 3) Download the Christian Vitality Prayer PDF.

Step 4) Download the Christian Vitality Prayer MP3.

Step 5) Schedule time first thing in the morning and the last thing at night so you can spend three to five minutes going through the prayer. The MP3 is great for this!

Step 6) Share the Christian Vitality Prayer with your spouse, and start praying together regularly (studies show spouses who pray together reduce their divorce rate from 50% to less than 1%).

Step 7) Share the prayer with your family and friends.

Step 8) Get even more out of the program by joining the Christian Vitality Prayer - Private Membership Program

As I mentioned in the preface of this book, please do me the honor of sharing this little book/program with as many of your family and friends as you can. Your personal testimony of how it has transformed your prayer life and life overall is the greatest tool for me to make the body of believers aware of this tremendous blessing I call the Christian Vitality Prayer. If you deem it worthy of such a high compliment, please purchase them an Amazon gift card to buy their own copy. I will be keeping the price as low as I can to cover the costs of getting the word out, so a couple of dollars that could change the lives of your family and friends should be a no-brainer investment. **Together we can start a revival in the body of believers that will help us achieve the great commission in a bigger and better way. Thank you!**

May you encounter God every day and experience synchronicity, oneness, and awareness of God's perfect will for your life and make leaps and bounds of progress towards it's attainment for your life. In the name of Jesus Christ our wonderful Lord and Savior. AMEN!

Sincerely and faithfully your brother in Christ,

~ Pastor Dan

CHAPTER 8. WHAT TO DO ONCE YOU RECEIVE YOUR BIG DREAM

BELIEVE & RECEIVE YOUR BIG DREAM

What's your big dream?

In the Christian Vitality Prayer Book there are several references to my sincere desire that "God would instill and awaken a dream so Big for your life that only God can make it happen".

So, after you've been using the prayer consistently and practicing real-time living, the semblance of a big dream is starting to rise up in your soul. Maybe God has even brought you to a place where you know what your big dream is. Now what?

The problem you may be experimenting now--and it's only human--is that this dream is way too big for you. It's hard to believe. You start to take control of the dream and take ownership of it, and it becomes overwhelming. You start thinking this is way too big for you to handle. Where do you start? What do you do next? We start to think it's all up to us. We put God in a box and start to think that this is impossible.

In the chapter on real-time living, I warned you to not take trips into the future without God by your side. You'll have to do this throughout your walk towards your dream--but live real time. Ask God what the next step is in prayer, and just take the next (much smaller) step towards the attainment of your dream. One step at a time. Baby steps.

What you don't realize now that will only become clear to you when you look back on this sometime in the future is that the dream God has for your life is so much bigger than you can even imagine. Imagine, for example, a large landscape puzzle with 28,854 pieces--one piece for each day of the average seventy-nine-year human lifespan (in America currently). The overall puzzle is something you could never comprehend, and the funny thing is that by our obedient actions and prosperity from those actions, you have an impact on how beautiful a landscape God can create with your life.

I never dreamed even a year ago that I'd have a published book--especially this book, one with Prayer in the title of it. Several years ago I started praying the Christian Vitality Prayer before it even had a name. I did so for many years before I even started down this path of empowering other believers. Slowly, however, God started to awaken and instill a dream for my life. He only revealed brief glimpses at first. He would shed just enough light on my life that I could take that next step. As I took that last step, he then started to shed more light for the next step. I had no idea I was heading here.

I was just obedient to the call in the moment on a daily basis. Sure there were days when life (and sin) got me off track as I was just as disobedient as the next person. But I always remembered what a pastor told me years ago: "Keep doing the last thing God told you to do until he tells you something different."

In prayer and meditation on his word, surrender to the Holy Spirit and communicate with God. Practice listening for his still, small voice. Isolate yourself for brief periods of time to steal away from life (quiet time in prayer like Jesus often did away from distractions) and listen for his still, small voice. You'll know in your heart what the next step is.

When you do hear his still, small voice, take action on that step. Keep doing that until he tells you something different.

When you find yourself feeling lost and confused as to what to do next, it may be sin that has caused a separation between you and God, and you will find you are not hearing his voice. Confess your sin in the moment and receive forgiveness, and be healed. Go back to God in prayer and supplication (submit to him) and listen for the next thing to do. If there isn't a new revelation after prayer, then stay the course. Keep doing that last thing God told you to do until he tells you something different.

God will work out the details along the way. Your job is to commit and surrender the dream to him daily. Take the next step you feel led to take, and surrender the rest to him.

I once shared a message with my church on God's providence many years ago. I summed up the entire message with this analogy. When God asks you to do something, you just have to say, "Yes Lord," and take that first step, just like Moses putting his staff in the river and taking the first step in.

I told them to imagine for a moment that God asked them to cross a lake that is covered by a thick layer of fog at the moment and you can't see farther than a boat length into the fog. You don't know exactly where God wants you to land on the other side of that lake or even how big this lake is. All you see is a motor boat parked on the shore right next to you. You don't know what lies ahead, if there are obstacles in the lake that could sink your little boat, or even the exact course. God just asked you to get in the boat, start the motor, and begin crossing.

God's providence is like a wind that he will use to blow you on the course he wants you on. Your only requirement at the moment is that you take that first step and get into the boat. The next step is to start the motor. Then put the motor in drive and start going forward. God will direct your path, and you will land where he wants you to land. But none of this will happen unless you take that first step into the boat.

That first step and all that follow require a degree of faith from you. You have to trust that God is your source and is interested in every detail of your life. He will direct you where he wants you to go, but it is our cooperative effort of taking action towards the goal of crossing the lake even when we don't clearly see where we are heading that makes all the difference in the world.

This book itself is evidence of part of my personal Big Dream. Over the last couple of years God has directed me down this path to a new mission for my life: "Empowering Revival in the lives of Christians Worldwide by teaching, inspiring, and empowering believers with the practical application of Modern Science and Biblical Wisdom."

I find myself today with the book published and ready for people to discover it…read it…put it into practice…and to ultimately experience their own personal revivals. I am personally powerless over what happens next and am completely dependent upon God to provide. He is my source and supply, and all my needs are met by him. The book now feels as if it is his personal challenge to me of whether I believe what I actually wrote.

I do sincerely believe the content in this book, and I surrender myself and this book to him. "Everything over which you've given me authority, Lord, I place at your feet" (from the Christian Vitality Prayer). "I place the Christian Vitality Prayer Book at your feet Lord" is my prayer.

I find myself across the lake and landed on the shore with the completion of this book. It's time now for quiet time again in prayer, to ask, "What's next Papa?" I can't take ownership of what happens next. It's up to him who and reads the book, and it's up to you, the reader, to start your own journey. What I do know is this:

I believe that Jesus is the Son of God.

I believe that he died on the cross for my sins and rose again securing my salvation.

I believe that he who lives inside of me now is greater than he that is in control of the world.

I believe that nothing is impossible to him (me) that believes.

I believe that God loves me and is interested in every detail of my life.

I believe that he called me to write the Christian Vitality Prayer book and that it is an imperfect work written by man (me), but that it was inspired by God's Holy Spirit and can and will be used for his purposes on earth.

I believe the universe benefits directly and indirectly by the value added by my obedient actions and prosperity. This book is evidence of my obedient actions, that God will bless the work, and that the universe (man specifically) will benefit directly and indirectly by my actions of writing and promoting it.

I commit and surrender this goal/dream of having thousands (or even millions) of people being blessed by what I've written to him today. That the Christian Vitality Prayer book would become a best seller some day and be a blessing to anyone that reads it. That it would be a catalyst to change people's lives and awaken big dreams in anyone who reads it. That it would start a revival in the body of believers and be used to extend God's presence in more human lives. That you and I would spark a revival of lost souls and have a significant impact on the attainment of God's perfect will for the human race.

Would you please join me, sister or brother, in this short prayer?

Dear Father, I release this book to you in the name of Jesus Christ your wonderful Son and my best friend. May your Holy Spirit speak through my words, and may your living word that I have quoted inspire the readers of this book in such a way as to spark a revival in their lives and the lives of their family and friends. You promised, Lord, that your word will not return void. I claim that promise now for the Christian Vitality Prayer book.

In Jesus' Name, AMEN!

Thank you, dear friend!

It's your turn now to join me in asking, "What's next Papa?"

About the Author

Pastor Dan Matejsek is the founder and president of Christian Vitality LLC, an international organization dedicated to fostering revival in the lives of Christians worldwide through teaching, inspiring, and empowering believers with the practical application of Modern Science and Biblical Wisdom. He lives in Scottsdale, Arizona with his wife, Diana, and five children.

Find out more at christianvitality.com/about-us/

Can I Ask A Favor?

If you enjoyed this book, found it useful or otherwise, I'd really appreciate it if you would post a short review on Amazon. I do read all the reviews personally so that I can continually write what people are wanting.

If you'd like to leave a review, please visit the link below:

[Click Here Be Awesome And Leave An Honest Review](#)

Thanks for your support!

~ Pastor Dan

P.S. Please also copy your review in the Facebook page here:

[facebook.com/ChristianVitalityPrayerBook](#)

READ THESE OTHER PRAYER BOOKS

(Visit the Google Shortcut below the Author's name)

Prayer: Experiencing Awe and Intimacy with God
by Timothy Keller
http://goo.gl/IK7Wy6

Prayer
by Philip Kerr
http://goo.gl/v6u734

Prayer
by Philip Yancey
http://goo.gl/JKZo0i

Prayer: The Ultimate Conversation
by Charles F. Stanley
http://goo.gl/ZW9D16

Prayer: Our Deepest Longing
by Ronald Rolheiser
http://goo.gl/3X9Mw6

Prayer: Finding the Heart's True Home
by Richard J. Foster
http://goo.gl/V2Pvde

Before Amen: The Power of a Simple Prayer
Max Lucado
http://goo.gl/T8Waa7